The Original Book of HORSE TREATS

Photo contributed by Bonnie Kreitler. © Kreitler Media Services

The Original Book of HORSE TREATS

Recipes you can make at home for your horse!

Including Hors(e) d'Oeuvres, Salads, Snacks, Bran Mashes, Desserts, Natural Remedies and Treatments, and more.

Compiled & Illustrated by
June V. Evers

Published by
Horse Hollow Press, Inc.
© 1994

Thank you to everyone who helped me with this book—especially all the people who sent
in their recipes and pictures. Thank you for expressing as much excitement about the project as I did.
Thank you to my Mom and the use of her kitchen, which I took over to test the recipes.
Thank you Dad and my brother, Charles.
Thank you to Jim K. for all his valuable insight and information.
Thank you Kathy F. and Dick H.
Thank you to all our pals at Grandmas® Molasses.
Thank you to the gang at Atwater Press
and everyone whose support and guidance made this book possible.
And thank you to the horses who tested the recipes.

Stable of Contents

　　　• Electrolytes • feed additives
　　　• Liniments • hoof care • detanglers • fly sprays • heel scratch preparation
　　　• Colic elixirs • administering medicines

One day last spring when I was making my horse's favorite bran mash, I began to wonder if other owners enjoyed preparing treats for their horses as much as I did. I placed a number of telephone calls to friends and found that yes, indeed, their horses were also pampered regularly with homemade treats lovingly served up.

From this, the idea for **The Original Book of Horse Treats** was born. The first "call for recipes" soon went out in a number of magazines across the country, thanks to the generous help of the publishers and editors in charge. The response from readers was terrific!

I would like to thank everyone who took the time to send me their favorite homemade treats and, in many cases, photos of their horses. I've included as many recipes as I could in their original form, but through testing, some needed to be edited slightly to better balance the recipe or to comply with our veterinarian's advice. I regret that I have not been able to print every recipe and every photo.

My horse Mary Ellen (that's her on the right) would also express her gratitude if only she could keep her nose out of the feed bucket long enough. As the official taster for **The Original Book of Horse Treats**, it's safe to say that she's been absolutely delighted with everyone's culinary contributions during the past several months.

I'm very pleased to present this book for all horse lovers and their horses. I'm sure you'll enjoy preparing and serving these treats for your horse as much as I did for mine.

June V. Evers
Goshen, New York

The happiest horse in America

The author's horse, Mary Ellen, daintily taste-testing yet another treat out of a bowl.

Photo contributed by Bonnie Kreitler. © Kreitler Media Services

Dear Reader,

Horse Hollow Press is proud to present **The Original Book of Horse Treats.** We're sure it will bring you and your horse years of pleasure and enjoyment.

It is important to note that these recipes are meant to be served as *occasional* treats (bran mashes, for example, should not usually be fed to horses more than once a week), and are not intended to be substitutes or replacements for your horse's normal daily feed. And, while the ingredients in these recipes are foods commonly fed to horses, the publisher recommends that you check with your veterinarian first (as you should with any diet changes) before you serve any of these treats to your horse. Also, if your horse bolts his feed (eats too quickly), replace small hard candy garnishes such as peppermints and jelly beans, with grapes or the other mushier garnishes suggested in the Decorative Garnishes section, page 61. We expect you to use your own good judgment on the horse receiving the treats. And, if a small horse or pony is receiving the treats, check with your veterinarian and adjust the quantity to fit your horse or pony.

Regarding the remedies for colic on page 70, the publisher emphasizes that veterinarian care remains *the best and preferred* treatment for colic. These homemade remedies, while used successfully for years by those individuals who contributed them for this book, are not offered as substitutes for experienced veterinary care. Again, we recommend that you always check with your veterinarian before you administer these or any other homemade colic remedy.

These recommendations aside, it is our pleasure to share with you what other horse lovers from all over the United States, Canada and Mexico have so generously shared with us. These fabulous treats are so much fun to make and even more fun to serve — and your horse will absolutely love them. **Enjoy!**

—Horse Hollow Press

Photo courtesy of Falabella Limited Collection Sale and contributed by Horse Play magazine of Gaithersburg, MD.

Hors(e) d'Oeuvres

Lancer during his workout, Goshen, NY.

Stuffed Molasses Apples

Ingredients:

- **2 apples**
- **1 cup bran**
- **1 carrot, shredded**
- **3/4 cup molasses**
- **1/2 cup brown sugar**
- **1/2 cup sweet feed**
- **2 sprigs of parsley or green carrot top**
- **2 seedless green grapes**
- **Confectionery sugar**

Core two apples and dig out as much of the center as you can, as you would a pumpkin at Halloween. Set this aside.

Mix shredded carrot with bran, molasses, brown sugar and sweet feed in a large bowl. Add more molasses or bran to give mixture a stiff consistency. Scoop mixture out of the bowl and press into cored apples. Press fairly tightly.

To garnish: Drip a small amount of molasses over the top so it runs down sides of the apple. Add a sprig of parsley or carrot greens, top with a green seedless grape, sprinkle with confectionery sugar and serve immediately! Serve in a feed bucket as this is a gooey treat. Serves two horses.

Or serve: After you've cored apple, slice in half and press ingredients into each half, garnish as in the whole apple recipe and serve four horses.

Super suggestion: Terrific for hiding worming medication or other veterinarian prescribed medicines. ♥

Carrot-Apple Pâté with Faux Caviar

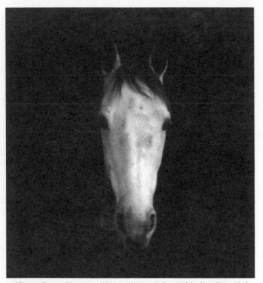

Killarney County Kerry owned by Mr. & Mrs. Robert Holzhacker of New York City. Mrs. Holzhacker snapped this ghostly photo one night after riding.

Ingredients:

2 carrots, diced

1 apple, sliced

1/3 cup honey (or molasses)

1/3 cup bran

1/4 cup water

Hay cubes

Handful of horse feed pellets

Handful of raisins

Place apples, honey (or molasses), bran and water into a blender. Add carrots slowly and blend until puréed. Mixture should be pasty; add more bran if necessary. Spread liberally onto each hay cube and top with one raisin and a sprinkle of pellets ("faux caviar"). ♥

Contributed by Helen Zahrndt of Spencer, SD. Helen noted her horses love this delectable treat on Sunday afternoons as an appetizer before their dinner.

Sonny's Apples

Ingredients:

4 Macintosh apples

1/2 cup corn syrup

Peel and quarter apples. Place in a feed bucket and pour syrup over the apples and serve. ♥

Contributed by Jane Berg of Margate, FL. Jane is a volunteer with Horses and Handicapped of South Florida, a therapeutic riding program that helps build self-esteem, self-discipline, coordination, balance, muscle tone and strength of riders with a variety of disabilities. What a wonderful program—to bring horses together with children and adults who need them. Sonny is one of their horses.

SEE SECTION ON DECORATIVE GARNISHES, PAGE 61, FOR SUGGESTIONS ON HOW TO USE THE PEELS LEFT OVER FROM THE ABOVE RECIPE.

Rolled Carrot Nibbles

Ingredients:

3 carrots with the green tops

1/3 cup cracked corn or feed

1/4 cup molasses

Brown sugar

ut up carrots into 3-inch pieces. Cut carrot tops off but don't throw them away. Set all aside.

Cow pony in a field near Crowheart, Wyoming.

Pour molasses onto a plate with a lip. Mix in enough brown sugar, about 1 to 3 tablespoons, to thicken the molasses. Onto another plate, spread feed or cracked corn.

Roll carrots in the molasses mixture until they are completely covered. Then, roll carrots in the feed or cracked corn. Place rolled carrots directly in feed bucket. Wrap the carrot tops around carrots, for a delicious additive to a sweet treat. If you have extra sauce, dribble over the top of treat.

Super clean up suggestion: Make this recipe directly in the feed bucket. Mix the molasses and brown sugar on the right hand side of the feed bucket, place the grain on the left. Do your mixing and rolling directly in the bucket. It saves on clean up and your horse will lick his bucket clean. ♥

Super Supper Suggestion:

MIX CRACKED CORN OR FEED WITH BROWN SUGAR AND MOLASSES IN A BOWL. PLACE A FLAKE OF HAY IN YOUR HORSE'S STALL OR PASTURE. MAKE SURE FLAKE IS FLAT ON GROUND OR FLAT IN FEED BUCKET. PLACE CARROTS ON THE HAY AND THEN DRIBBLE THE MIXTURE OVER THE CARROTS, LETTING JUST A BIT ONTO THE HAY *(NOT TOO MUCH, AS YOU DON'T WANT YOUR HORSE PICKING UP TOO MUCH DIRT OR BEDDING)*. GARNISH WITH CARROT TOPS.

Biscuit Mix

Ingredients:

- 10 cups flour
- 1 2/3 cups instant nonfat dry milk
- 1/3 cup baking powder
- 2 1/2 teaspoons salt
- 1 2/3 cups shortening

Combine dry ingredients in a large tupperware container (6 to 8 quarts) that can be covered and refrigerated. Add shortening and mix with a blender or mixer until shortening is well dispersed and mixture looks like fine crumbs. Store tightly covered in the refrigerator. It will last about 3 months. Makes about 15 cups of biscuit mix. ♥

Miss Koko's Biscuits

Ingredients:

- 3 cups Biscuit Mix (see recipe at left)
- 1 or 2 carrots, coarsely grated
- 2/3 cup water
- 1/4 cup sugar (optional)

Preheat oven to 425 degrees. Combine Biscuit Mix, carrots and sugar in a large bowl. Gradually add water to make dough soft but not sticky. Knead dough on a lightly floured board about 15 times. Divide dough in half and roll each section out flat, about 1/4 inch thick. Cut with a 2-inch-round biscuit cutter or cookie cutter. Bake until lightly browned, about 10 minutes. Makes 40 biscuits. ♥

Biscuit Mix and Miss Koko's Biscuits contributed by Roseanne Slivak, who operates Horse'N Around Tack Shop, Inc. at Mt. Pleasant Quarter Horse Farm in Sewell, NJ. She says her mother, Mrs. Jean Slivak, makes these biscuits for an elderly pony named Miss Koko. Miss Koko has been adopted as the mascot of Horse'N Around Tack Shop. Miss Koko loves these treats and looks forward to them every week!

Carrot Rumaki

Ingredients:

1 carrot, shredded

1/4 cup brown sugar

1/4 cup bran

1/4 cup sweet feed

1/4 cup dark corn syrup

Iceberg lettuce

4 pieces of hay, pick the stiffest pieces
    from a flake and cut to
    5 inches long

Use the dark green leaves of the iceberg lettuce. If they are a *little* limp that is best. Tear off 4 large leaves and set aside. Return the head of lettuce back to the refrigerator.

Paint mare enjoying a lush pasture. Photo contributed by Bonnie Kreitler.
© Kreitler Media Services

In a separate bowl, mix all ingredients together. Make sure mixture is moist but not runny, by adding more syrup or bran if necessary.

Lay a lettuce leaf flat, place about 1/2 cup of mixture in a mound on the leaf. Roll leaf around mixture, until it is shaped like a tube. Pierce from the side with a piece of hay. Makes four Rumaki hors(e) d' oeuvres. ♥

Carrot Crispies

Ingredients:

2 carrots, shredded

1 apple, chopped in small pieces

1/3 cup molasses

1/2 to 3/4 cup bran

Triscuits (or other salty crackers)

Combine carrots, apple, molasses and bran, mix thoroughly. Scoop a small ball onto Triscuits and refrigerate overnight. Carrot Crispies will hold their shape if they are kept cool, but be careful: they get somewhat crumbly at room temperature. Makes six to ten crackers. ♥

Based on a recipe by Elizabeth Sutton and Meghan Pomeroy of Ontario, Canada.

Mary Ellen looks into the barn as we fix her favorite salad. Photo contributed by Suzanne DeMarco of Warwick, NY.

Soups, Stews & Salads

Satin Lady and Lincoln on a St. Remy, New York horse farm. Photo contributed by Lisa Sammens of Hurley, NY.

Alfalfa Soup

Ingredients:

Alfalfa hay cubes

1 cup mineral oil or corn oil

1 to 2 gallons of hot water

ill a 5 gallon feed bucket 1/4 to 1/3 full of loose alfalfa cubes. Mix the cubes and 1 gallon of hot water. Let sit for 20 minutes and add the oil. Add more warm water if necessary to make a thick soup. Make sure it is warm and not hot before you feed. ♥

Contributed by Jane Berg of Margate, FL. Jane is a volunteer with Horses and Handicapped of South Florida.

IF YOUR HORSE IS NOT ACCUSTOMED TO ALFALFA CUBES, GRADUALLY INTRODUCE THIS RECIPE WITH A VERY SMALL QUANTITY.

Cowboy's Stew

Ingredients:

3 pounds carrots, shredded

2 cups sweet feed

2 cups oats

1 flake of timothy alfalfa mix hay

n a blender, gradually blend carrots, adding about 1/2 cup of water to help it blend. Place into a big bowl. Add sweet feed and oats, mix thoroughly.

Put a flake of hay in feed bucket and pour the mixture over the top as a garnish. ♥

Contributed also by Jane Berg. The stew is named for Cowboy, a horse in the Horses and Handicapped of South Florida program.

Corn Silk Salad

Ingredients:

2 whole ears of fresh corn, husks and silk

1 red onion sliced

1 apple, quartered

2 pears, quartered

2 broccoli spears

reak ears of corn in halves, leave silk and husks on the corn. Toss all ingredients together in a feed bucket. *To garnish:* Sprinkle salad with corn oil. ♥

Contributed by Lorraine Harwelik, owner of the Equestrian's Pro Shop in Linden, NJ.

ANOTHER SUGGESTION: CUT UP CANTALOUPE, HONEY DEW AND WATERMELONS, LEAVING SKIN AND SEEDS. ADD 1/2 TO 3/4 CUP OF SHELLED SUNFLOWER SEEDS.

Contributed also by Lorraine Harwelik, owner of the Equestrian's Pro Shop in Linden, NJ.

Christmas Salad

Ingredients:

- 6 apples, quartered
- 8 carrots, cut in 3 inch pieces
- 2 cups Quaker Oats
- 1 cup sweet feed
- Molasses

ombine all ingredients together and fold in enough molasses to make the oatmeal and grain stick to the fruit. Chill overnight and serve on Christmas morning. ♥

Contributed by June Laughlin of Bedford, VA.

SUBSTITUTE YOUR OWN HORSE'S FEED WHEN RECIPE CALLS FOR OATS OR SWEET FEED!

Foxi's Cheap & Easy Horse Croutons

Ingredients:

- Leftover bread
- 1/4 cup honey or molasses
- 1/4 cup water
- Granulated sugar

reheat oven to 450 degrees. Lightly grease cookie sheet or aluminum foil.

Cut up leftover bread (any kind) into cubes, about 1 inch by 1 inch, and put in large bowl. In a separate bowl, mix honey or molasses with water. Sprinkle the diluted honey/molasses mixture on cubes and toss together until well moistened, but not soggy. Spread cubes on cookie sheet and sprinkle with sugar.

Place in oven and turn down to 200 degrees. Leave in the oven for several hours until toasted, stirring occasionally. Turn off oven and leave cubes in the oven overnight. Ready to feed the next day. ♥

Contributed by Judith Streisand, MD, of Glen Head, NY.

Tri-Color Apple & Carrot Salad

Ingredients:

- 1 large handful of hay
- 1 to 2 carrots with the tops, sliced
- 2 red apples, cut in sixths
- 2 green apples, cut in sixths
- 2 yellow apples, cut in sixths

Straighten out hay and cut with scissors into pieces approximately 10 inches long and place in feed bucket. Arrange in a crisscross pattern, making a circle flat on the bottom of the feed bucket. Cut the tops off the carrots and tuck the green tops in around the edge of the crisscrossed hay.

Arrange sliced carrots and the apples in a decorative manner, alternating colors, as in diagram above.

To garnish: Place a sprig of carrot top in the center of the salad. ❤

Spring Salad

Ingredients:

- Green carrot tops, cut from 3 carrots
- 6 pea pods
- Green beet tops, cut from 1 beet

Toss greens together and feed as an appetizer before or on top of grain. As an added touch, dress with corn oil. ❤

Contributed by Julie Salisbury of Canada.

Photo contributed by Lesley Ward, Editor of Young Rider Magazine of Williamsburg, VA.

Bran Mashes

Belgians at a sleigh rally. Photo contributed by Stephanie Macejko. Stephanie is the Editor of Just About Horses, the magazine for Breyer Animal Creations.

Sam Savitt's Cold Winter Evening Bran Mash

Ingredients:

4 cups sweet feed

6 cups bran

1 cup molasses

Hot water

mix sweet feed with the bran. Add hot water until it is the consistency of hamburger. Then add 1 cup of molasses. Let steep for 5 to 10 minutes. ♥

Contributed by Sam Savitt, world famous equestrian artist and author. He has 15 books to his credit, as well as fabulously illustrated commissioned works of art and educational posters. He resides with his wife, Bette, in North Salem, NY.

IF YOU'RE ADDING GRAIN, NEVER ADD MORE THAN YOU NORMALLY SERVE YOUR HORSE.

❊

BRAN MASHES ARE A TERRIFIC WAY TO FEED ORAL MEDICATIONS, SUCH AS BUTE OR WORMERS!

"On a cold winter evening, there is nothing like a hot mash. Picture this—the horses are in their stalls waiting. They seem to know what's coming. They nicker softly asking me to hurry. I mix one third-sweet feed to two thirds-bran. As the hot water goes in I keep mixing with a short stick until it is the consistency of hamburger. To this mixture, I add about a cup of molasses. At this point, it smells so good I could eat it myself. The horses nicker louder as I come in and dump this delicious concoction in their feeders. Then I sit on the feed bin and listen to them munch away—greatest sound in the world." —Sam Savitt

Breeze's Bran Mash Ecstasy

Ingredients:

4 cups bran

1 cup Cheerios cereal

1 cup Quaker Oat Bran cereal

1 cup Corn Chex cereal

1/2 cup Quaker Oats

6 carrots, cut into 3 inch pieces

1 apple, cut in quarters

1 jar junior baby food fruit

(applesauce, pears, apricots

or peaches)

Hot water

in a large mixing bowl or feed bucket, combine all dry ingredients with enough hot water to create a moist mash. Cover with towel for 3 to 5 minutes and stir in carrots, fruit, and baby food fruit. Add more warm water if necessary and stir. Feed immediately.

Super summer suggestion: Add green or red seedless grapes with other fruit. ❤

Contributed by Mary E. Welch of Lawrenceville, GA. Mary noted in her letter to us that her thoroughbred, Aruba Breeze, receives this delectable bran mash treat every Wednesday and boy, does he love it!

WHOA! *Important Note:*

BRAN MASHES SHOULD BE FED *ONLY*

ONCE A WEEK.

It was brought to our attention while compiling this book that a small amount of bran can be fed every day, BUT it should be <u>gradually</u> introduced to be fed daily. Remember, bran is a laxative.

❋

IF YOUR HORSE DOES NOT EAT ALL

OF HIS MASH, *DON'T SAVE IT FOR LATER!*

Mashes ferment and can make a horse sick. Always clean out his feed bucket and throw the uneaten portion away.

❋

THE AMOUNT OF DRY BRAN CAN VARY

DEPENDING ON THE SIZE OF YOUR HORSE.

Mary Ellen, our 1000 lb. horse receives 8-12 cups of bran for her once-a-week bran mash treat. Ponies and smaller horses: reduce portions and consult with your veterinarian!

A Dash of Christmas Mash

Ingredients:

6 cups of cob

Cob is a mixture of corn, oats and barley (or your horse's regular feed)

1 1/2 cups bran

1 apple, cut in quarters

3 carrots, sliced

1/2 cup molasses

Hot water

place ingredients in a feed bucket. Pour on enough hot water to just cover all ingredients. Cover bucket with a towel and let steam until cool enough to eat, but still warm. Remove towel and mix thoroughly. ❤

Contributed by Terri Kistler, Whistlekick Ranch of Coos Bay, OR. Terri says she feeds this to her horses — Shorty, Tess, and Magnum — at Christmas and every time the weather gets cold.

Rejuvenating Bran Mash for Older Horses

Ingredients:

8 to 10 cups bran

2 carrots, grated

2 apples, finely chopped

4 tablespoons salt

2 cups molasses

1 cup brown sugar

Hot water

i n a feed bucket, dilute salt, molasses, and brown sugar with 1 gallon hot water. Add the bran, carrots, apples and mix well. Add more hot water, if necessary. Let steep 5 to 10 minutes and feed warm.

Older horses do not like to drink ice-cold water in the winter and have a tendency to become dehydrated. This mash, made soupy with extra water, will enable your older horse to get more fluids. ♥

19-year-old Mary Ellen hears her favorite sound: the feed buckets rattling with bran mash preparation. She receives this mash every Sunday.

Merlin. Photo contributed by Sallie Scoggin of Chicago, IL.

Classic Bran Mash

Ingredients:

- 6 cups bran
- 6 cups sweet feed
- 1/8 cup salt
- 1 cup molasses
- 2 carrots, sliced
- 1 apple, quartered
- Handful of sugar cubes
- Hot water

 ix bran and sweet feed together in a feed bucket. Add hot water until the mixture resembles pea soup. Add more water or bran to make it thicker or thinner. After this is mixed, add salt, carrots, apples and sugar cubes. Then, dribble molasses over the top as an icing. Let steep until cool enough to eat. ♥

Contributed by Linda Abrams, Pegasus Place School of Riding & Driving, Inc., of Milner, GA. Linda has been a riding instructor for 34 years. She has written articles for notable magazines such as the Chronicle of the Horse.

Bran Mash Purée Supreme

Ingredients:

- 2 cups applesauce
- 3 carrots, chopped finely for blender
- 1 cup molasses
- 1 cup brown sugar
- 6 to 8 cups bran
- 4 cups sweet feed
- Sprig green carrot top
- Hot water

p ut bran and sweet feed into a feed bucket and set aside.

In a blender, purée molasses, brown sugar, applesauce and 1 cup hot water. Add carrots slowly and carefully blend. Pour blended mixture into the feed bucket, over bran and sweet feed, and mix thoroughly. Add more hot water to make a mash resembling a thin oatmeal.

To garnish: Place a sprig of carrot top in the center. Slice another apple in quarters and place pieces around carrot top green in center. Let mash steep until cool enough to eat.

Super suggestion: This is an especially sweet mash, great for hiding worming medication. ♥

FOR EASTER, TOP BRAN MASH WITH

A HANDFUL OF JELLY BEANS.

Contributed by Karen Ufret of Port Jervis, NY. Karen notes her horses love the jelly beans just as a plain treat. Karen owns a pinto mare who is just about to foal.

INSTEAD OF ADDING MOLASSES TO SWEETEN

BRAN MASHES, TRY HONEY OR PANCAKE SYRUP!

Contributed by Anita Cantor of Paradise Valley, CA.

Bucket Lickin' Bran Mash

Photo contributed by Lesley Ward of Young Rider Magazine.

FOR AN INTERESTING CHANGE, ADD APPLE SAUCE INSTEAD OF CARROTS AND APPLES.

Ingredients:

8 cups bran
1 cup rolled oats
1/4 cup vegetable oil
1/4 cup molasses
1 1/2 cups hot water
1 carrot, sliced
1 apple, sliced

ix bran and oats with hot water, then add oil and molasses. This is a drier mash, so add more water if you like it soupier. Cover and let steep until cool enough to eat. ❤

Contributed by Martha Little of Chiloquin, OR. Martha says that she serves her bran mash treat every Sunday night.

IF A RECIPE SUGGESTS A FEED OR GRAIN THAT YOUR HORSE IS NOT ACCUSTOMED TO, SUBSTITUTE YOUR OWN GRAIN!

When starting any new feed, gradually introduce it, until your horse is used to it.

Additional additives to bran mashes:

1. **SALT — 2 TABLESPOONS TO 1/8 CUP.**

2. **ELECTROLYTES — FOLLOW DIRECTIONS ON THE JAR.**

3. **ADD 1 CUP SOY BEAN MEAL FOR WEIGHT GAIN.**

4. **ADD 1/3 CUP OF CORN OIL FOR GOOD COAT AND SHINE, OR MINERAL OIL IF YOU LIVE IN SANDY AREAS FOR COLIC PREVENTION.**

Contributed by Marguerite Porter of Peyton, CO.

5. **ADD 2 TABLESPOONS OF GROUND SAGE.**

6. **ADD 1 TO 2 CLOVES CRUSHED GARLIC.**

Contributed by Gladys Bernstein of Fort Lee, NJ.

(Be sure to check with your vet whether these are appropriate for your horse.)

❋

WHOA!
Important Note:

WHEN IS BRAN TOO OLD TO FEED?
When you pick up a handful and the bran flakes hold together with a cobweb-like dust.

Quick 'n Easy Bran Mash

Ingredients:

- 8 cups bran
- 4 cups oats
- 4 carrots, sliced
- Hot water

mix all ingredients and add hot water until all ingredients are moist. Cover with a towel for 5 minutes before serving. ❤

Contributed by Jolene Venables. Jolene is famous for her horse rescue operation, her monthly newsletter, Trail Tails, and her monthly magazine, Trail Tails Equestrian Magazine, all based in Canoga Park, CA. To help, call 818-349-4113.

*Chaz, an eleven-year-old Arabian.
Photo contributed by Jolene Venables.*

Arabian at Sussex County Horse Show. Photo contributed by Stephanie Macejko.

WE SUGGEST HOT TAP WATER
FOR BRAN MASHES!

By the time you get to the barn, it will have cooled enough to eat. Boiling water takes too long to cool and, besides, you may burn your hands. ALWAYS make sure it is cool enough for your horse. For a summer refresher, fix a cool mash, but not cold!

Cold Water Woes:

IF YOUR HORSE LIVES FAR FROM YOUR HOME, OR HIS STABLE DOESN'T HAVE HOT WATER, YOU CAN STILL MAKE HIS FAVORITE BRAN MASH.

USE A THERMOS. MIX HOT WATER AND SOLUBLE INGREDIENTS (NOT THE BRAN MASH OR FEED) TOGETHER AND PUT IN THERMOS. IF YOU WANT TO ADD CARROTS AND APPLES, CUT THEM UP AHEAD OF TIME AND PUT THEM IN A CONTAINER TO CARRY ALONG.

WHEN YOU GET TO THE BARN, MIX EVERY-THING TOGETHER AND FEED TO A HAPPY WAITING HORSE.

Contributed by Julia Maynard and Sunny of Massapequa, NY.

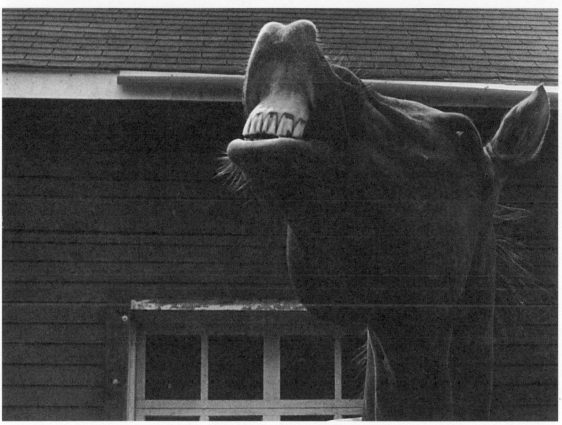

Backyard pal. Photo contributed by Elizabeth A. Fleck of Poughkeepsie, NY.

Beer Bran Mash

Ingredients:

8 cups bran

8 cups oats

Pinch of salt

Hot water

1 can of beer

add enough hot water to moisten ingredients, add a pinch of salt, mix and let steep for 30 minutes or until cool enough to eat. Before feeding, pour a can of fresh beer over the mash and feed. ♥

Contributed by Lura Bradbury Hyatt of Streetsboro, OH. This is an especially interesting recipe since the author's husband, the late Fred Bradbury, was a well-known racehorse trainer and driver in the 50's, 60's and 70's. She notes that Fred used this recipe for many years and would feed this mash to his horses after a demanding race.

Author's Note: I think it is fascinating to hear of old time recipes from the track and stables.

ANOTHER SUGGESTION:

USE 12 OZ. CAN OF GUINNESS STOUT INSTEAD OF REGULAR BEER.

Contributed by Lorraine Harwelik, owner of the Equestrian's Pro Shop in Linden, NJ.

Winter Tummy Warmer

Ingredients:

4 cups oats

3 cups bran

3 Uva Ursi leaves
   (available at health food stores)

1/2 teaspoon salt (add more if you like)

2 carrots, sliced

1 cup brown sugar

1 apple, quartered

Hot water

add enough hot water to all ingredients to make it moist. Let steep until cool enough to eat. For performance horses and horses who need to increase their water intake. ♥

Contributed by everyone at the Standardbred Retirement Foundation of Blairstown, NJ. The Foundation mentions that the Uva Ursi leaves are used frequently by Standardbred racehorse trainers. The leaves are a diuretic and, with the added salt, encourage a horse to drink a lot of water—especially in the winter. Plenty of fresh water should be available at all times with this recipe.

Partner In Crime in the Meadowlands stable area just prior to a race. Partner In Crime is now retired. He is one of the horses for whom the Standardbred Retirement Foundation will find a loving home. The Foundation has already placed over 100 horses. Standardbred horses are versatile, gentle and even-tempered. They are especially wonderful with children! To help: 908-362-9084. Photo contributed by the Standardbred Retirement Foundation of Blairstown, NJ.

BE SURE TO CHECK WITH YOUR VET BEFORE YOU FEED ANYTHING NEW TO YOUR HORSE.

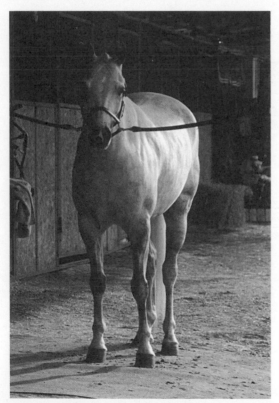

Well-groomed pony waiting his turn at a horse show. Photo contributed by Stephanie Macejko.

Epsom Salts Simple Mash

Ingredients:

- 8 cups bran
- 1 tablespoon salt
- 1 or 2 tablespoons Epsom salts
- Hot water

mix ingredients together. Add enough boiling hot water to make the mixture damp and clumpy, not soggy. Cover with a towel and let steep until cool enough to eat. ❤

Contributed by Kathy Andrews of Reidsville, NC, whose stable, Hunter Cross Farm, specializes in Hanoverians and Warmbloods. If your horse does not eat this bran mash because of the saltiness, add molasses, sweet feed or brown sugar. Epsom salts works as a laxative along with the bran.

SERVE BRAN MASH WARM, NEVER HOT.

(Super suggestion: Feed a cool mash in summer!)

❋

FEED A BRAN MASH TO MARES RIGHT

AFTER THEY HAVE FOALED.

Gatorade® Bran Mash

Ingredients:

- 4 cups sweet feed
- 8 cups bran
- 3 to 4 heaping tablespoons powdered lemon-lime Gatorade (use scoop provided in the container)
- Hot water

add enough hot water to all the ingredients to make them moist, let steep and feed warm.

Suggestion: Instead of water and powdered Gatorade, use bottled Gatorade (32 ounce jar). Mix in hot water as needed.

Another suggestion: If your horse has had an especially tiring day, instead of using electrolytes, pour the Gatorade directly into his water. Mix 3 to 5 heaping scoopfuls of the dry powder or a 32 ounce jar of premixed Gatorade into a 5-gallon bucket full of water. Horses love it so much they drink their water as if it was soda! ❤

Contributed by Lynn Borden of Middletown, NY. Her husband, Bruce, is a racehorse trainer and driver. Both have been in the business for over 20 years. Lynn says her horses don't like the orange Gatorade but love the lemon-lime!

BRAN MASHES ARE TERRIFIC WAY FOR

A HORSE TO GET WATER IF HE REFUSES TO

DRINK, ESPECIALLY IN THE WINTER.

JUST BE SURE TO MAKE IT SOUPY!

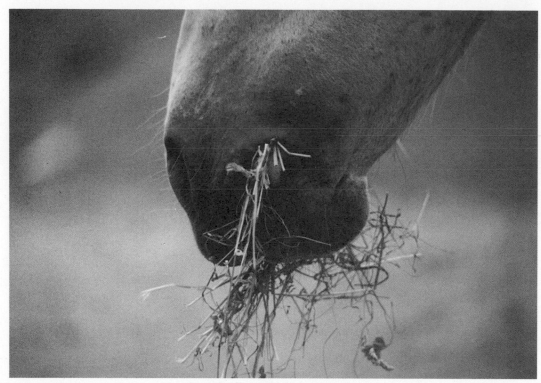

Ben munching. Photo contributed by Stephanie Macejko.

Snacks

Sweet Feed Quesadilla Surprise

Ingredients:

2 soft, flour tortillas

1 1/2 cups sweet feed

1 cup dark corn syrup

1/2 cup brown sugar

2 apples

1/2 cup flour

3/4 cup molasses

6 red seedless grapes

Sprig parsley

Carrot, cut in 3 inch strips

Slice 2 apples through the middle horizontally, so you have round slices about 1/4 inch thick. Set aside.

Mix sweet feed, corn syrup, brown sugar together well. Gradually add flour. Flour will thicken mixture, add more or less until desired consistency. Mixture should be very stiff, but not crumbly.

In the bottom of a feed bucket, lay 1 tortilla flat. Spread the prepared mixture evenly over the top of the tortilla and place the sliced apples flat on top. Cover with second tortilla.

In a separate bowl, mix the molasses and grapes together until grapes are coated and pour over the top of the tortilla.

To garnish: Place a sprig of parsley in the center and lay carrot strips around the perimeter of the feed bucket.

Super suggestion: To make a smaller serving, only use one tortilla. Place half the amount of ingredients onto half of the tortilla and fold over. Garnish as above. ♥

Apple Cider Pick-Me-Up

Ingredients:

1 cup apple cider (must be fresh— should not be old and fermented)

Just pour 1 cup directly into a clean feed bucket. If your horse does not immediately slurp this up, it must be cleaned out of his bucket. ♥

Contributed by Fay Seltzer, Hawk Shadow Feed & Saddlery of New Ringgold, PA.

Toast Nuggets

Ingredients:

1 piece of white or wheat bread
Strawberry, raspberry or grape jam
Sugar

toast the bread until it is crispy. Then spread jam thickly onto toast and sprinkle about a tablespoon of sugar on top. Cut into quarters and feed cool.

Super suggestion: This is a super and quick before-breakfast treat. Especially if your horse kicks or strikes his stall door for his food, this little treat will keep him busy while you are preparing his breakfast. ♥

Dream's Surprise

Ingredients:

6 carrots, sliced
2 cups dry oatmeal
1/2 cup molasses
1 1/2 cups applesauce

mix all ingredients together until coated in a feed bucket.

Super suggestion: Mix in 10 seedless green grapes and lightly sprinkle with 1/2 teaspoon cinnamon. ♥

Contributed by Chris Wegner of Wheaton, IL.

Pop Pop's Bonbons

Ingredients:

5 hay cubes
1/2 cup molasses
Sweet feed

pour molasses onto a plate with a lip. Roll hay cubes in molasses until they are completely covered, then sprinkle sweet feed over them — just enough to stick to the cubes as a garnish. ♥

Contributed by J. Burns of Hoboken, NJ. His horse, Pop Pop's Scooter, loves these treats.

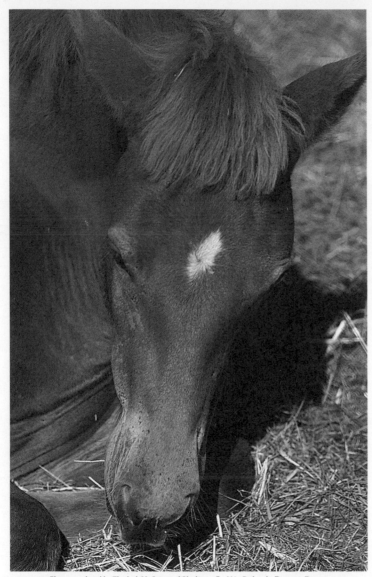

Photo contributed by Bonnie Kreitler. © Kreitler Media Services

Photo contributed by Elizabeth H. Sutton of Charlottesville, VA. Beth is the Executive Director of the Misty of Chincoteague Foundation, Inc. She is a well-known author and photographer as well!

Desserts

Above, Chincoteague ponies on Chincoteague Island, on Pony Penning Day.
Photos contributed by Elizabeth H. Sutton.

Misty II with Kerra Allen, daughter of Kendy Allen. Misty II carries on the tradition and the duties of her famous mother, Misty of Chincoteague.
Kendy Allen travels around the country to schools, telling the story of Misty and the Misty of Chincoteague Foundation.
Photo contributed by Kendy Allen of Manheim, PA.

Marguerite Henry's
Misty of Chincoteague Oat Cake

Ingredients:

- 2 1/4 cups flour
- 1 1/2 cups sugar
- 3 teaspoons baking powder
- 1 teaspoon salt
- 1 cup oats
- 1/2 cup shortening
- 2 egg yolks
- 2 egg whites
- 1 cup milk
- 1/4 cup finely chopped walnuts
- Molasses

preheat oven to 350 degrees. Grease and flour two 9-inch layer cake pans. Sift together: flour, sugar, baking powder and salt. Mix in oats. Add shortening. Beat egg yolks and milk. After well mixed, fold in egg whites.

Bake at 350 degrees for 35 to 40 minutes. Test with a toothpick. When cool, spread top with molasses and sprinkle with walnuts. For horses and people, too! ❤

Marguerite Henry's world-famous book about the real pony, Misty of Chincoteague, brought Misty and the wild ponies of Assateague into the nation's spotlight. Marguerite created and baked this very same cake for Misty's first birthday party.

In an interview with freelance equestrian journalist Holly Covey, Marguerite Henry mentioned that when Marguerite and Misty were promoting the Misty books, they once went to an American Library Association Convention and Misty rode up in an elevator at the convention center to meet the librarians.

The Misty of Chincoteague Foundation was created to raise money to buy the old Paul Beebe farm and land, where Misty was born. It will be restored as a museum to preserve the legend of Misty of Chincoteague. To help, contact: The Misty of Chincoteague Foundation, PO Box 4352, Charlottesville, VA 22905.

Recipe reprinted with the permission of Macmillan Publishing from A Pictorial Life Story of Misty by Marguerite Henry. Text copyright © 1976 Marguerite Henry. Reprinted by permission of Marguerite Henry and the Watkins/Loomis Agency.

Mary Ellen's "Fave" Carrot Cake

Ingredients:

- 1 cup sugar
- 1 cup light brown sugar
- 1 cup flour
- 1 cup bran
- 1 teaspoon baking powder
- 1 teaspoon baking soda
- 1 teaspoon cinnamon
- 3 cups carrots, shredded
- 1 1/2 cups corn oil
- 4 eggs
- 2 teaspoons vanilla
- 1 Macintosh apple, cut in sixths

 reheat oven to 325 degrees and grease a 13 x 9 inch baking pan.

In separate bowl, mix dry ingredients, then add carrots, oil, eggs and vanilla. Beat until mixed well and there are no lumps. Pour into prepared baking pans and bake for about 1 hour. Remove from pan when cool.

To Garnish: Slice an apple into sixths and arrange on top of cake, then sprinkle entire cake lightly with brown sugar. Serve cool. ❤

This is Mary Ellen's favorite and is reserved for birthdays!

Baba's Easy & Organic Carrot Cake

Ingredients:

- 12 carrots
- 1/2 cup brown sugar
- 2 apples, grated or finely chopped
- Sesame or flax seeds

take 12 carrots and run them through a vegetable juicer. Set the juice aside. Remove pulp from the juicer and place in a large bowl with brown sugar and apples. Add the juice only to moisten mixture. Press mixture firmly into a greased loaf pan and refrigerate 1 to 2 hours. Flip pan over and remove cake and garnish with a sprinkle of sesame or flax seeds. ❤

Contributed by Linda Stark of Gramercy Park, NYC. Linda frequently rides with Claremont Stables in Central Park.

Brown Sugar Peaches

Ingredients:

- 6 cups bran
- 6 cups Quaker Oats
- 4 fresh peaches, sliced
- 4 tablespoons brown sugar
- 1 tablespoon molasses
- 6 carrots, sliced
- 2 apples, quartered
- 1 cup corn oil
- Warm water

Preheat oven to 325 degrees. Grease a large baking pan and set aside.

Mix sliced apples with bran, Quaker Oats, 3 1/2 cups of warm water and molasses in a bowl. Pour mixture into baking pan. Bake for 25 to 30 minutes, and check often to make sure it is not getting too dark. Remove from the oven and let cool.

After it cools, place baked mixture directly into your horse's feed bucket with 2 1/2 to 3 cups of warm water and 1 cup corn oil. Mix thoroughly. Top with sliced carrots, sliced fresh peaches and sprinkle with brown sugar. ♥

Contributed by Margaret Walsh, Advertising Manager for Horse Show magazine, the magazine for American Horse Shows Association, New York City, NY. Margaret's horse, Donovan Dan, an appaloosa she's had for 14 years, absolutely loves this recipe.

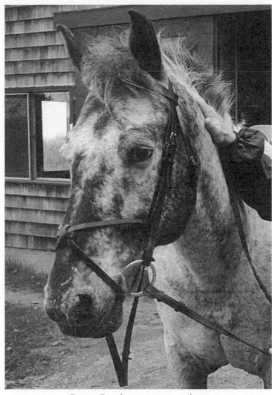
Donovan Dan after a cross-country work out.

Minced Treat

Ingredients:

15 pieces or stalks of hay

1 cup sugar

3 carrots, cut in 3 inch strips

cut stalks of hay with scissors into pieces 1 inch long and place into a cooking pot along with carrots. Add two cups of water and boil for 2 minutes. Drain off water, leaving about 1/2 cup in the pot. Stir the sugar into the mixture left in the pot and refrigerate until cool enough to eat. Scoop out directly into empty feed bucket or spread as an icing over grain. ♥

Contributed by Katy Koncen of St. Louis, MO.

Sweet Carrot Bundt

Ingredients:

Sweet feed

Corn syrup

Carrots with the green tops

use round baking pan approximately 3 to 4 inches deep and line with wax paper. In a separate bowl, use enough sweet feed to fill your baking pan to the top. Add enough corn syrup to moisten feed, but keep it sticky so you will be able to shape it. Press this mixture (rubbing a little corn oil on your hands will make this process a little easier) into the baking pan to fill it and refrigerate overnight.

When ready to use, remove cake from pan and peel off wax paper.

To garnish: Place cake onto a bed of green, leafy carrot tops and sprinkle cake top with grated or shredded carrot.

For an added touch on birthdays: Stick small carrots candles into the center. ♥

Contributed by Charleen Jones of Boonsboro, MD. She developed this cake to serve to Beau, the 30-year-old horse she has owned since he was a yearling.

Baked Carrot Crispies

Ingredients:

2 carrots, shredded

1 apple, shredded

1/3 cup molasses

1/4 cup bran

1/2 cup brown sugar

1/2 cup water

1/2 cup flour

1/4 cup dry oatmeal

Confectionery sugar

reheat oven to 400 degrees. Generously grease a muffin tin.

Mix carrots and apples in a bowl with molasses, bran, brown sugar, water, flour and oatmeal. Mixture should have a thick and doughy consistency. Add more bran if needed. Scoop dough into a muffin tin, sprinkle each muffin with brown sugar and bake in the oven for 30 to 50 minutes until cooked thoroughly. Let cool.

To garnish: Sprinkle lightly with confectionery sugar. Makes 6 muffins. ♥

Based on a recipe contributed by Elizabeth Sutton and Meghan Pomeroy of Ontario, Canada.

Sweet Success

Ingredients:

1 apple

1 carrot with the green tops

Molasses

ore the apple, making sure the hole is big enough to fit carrot through, so it sticks out both ends. Then dip it entirely into molasses and chill it until hard. Leave the green tops on the carrot as a decorative garnish. ♥

Contributed by Erin Appleyard of Ontario, Canada.

Christmas Pudding

Ingredients:

Magic Christmas Munchy Mixture
**Bread crumbs (make these by putting two
slices of bread into a blender)**
Parsley, celery leaves or carrot tops

Press as much Magic Christmas Munchy Mixture as you can firmly into a small round bowl, greased with corn oil. Place a plate over the top of the bowl and then tip the bowl over, holding the plate in place so the mixture doesn't fall out. Tap the bowl a few times and ease it off the pudding. You should have a perfectly shaped mound of Magic Christmas Munchy Mixture.

To garnish: Top with bread crumbs. Add some parsley, celery leaves or carrot tops around the base of the pudding. ♥

Contributed of Lesley Ward and Young Rider Magazine.

Magic Christmas Munchy Mixture

Use this as a base for the Christmas Pudding and Crunchy Christmas Cake

Ingredients:

2 to 4 cups feed (preferably coarse mix)
2 eggs
3 tablespoons molasses
1 to 1 1/2 cups hot water

Place feed in a large bowl. In a separate bowl, beat eggs well, add them to the feed, and mix well. Dissolve the molasses in hot water and add a little at a time to the feed mixture until it is sticky and firm. Pour it in gradually, as you may not need it all. You should be able to mold and shape the feed mix. Add more liquid or more feed for the correct consistency. This is the base for the Christmas Pudding and for the Munchy Crunchy Christmas Cake. ♥

Contributed by Lesley Ward of Williamsburg, VA and courtesy of Young Rider Magazine. Lesley is the Editor of Young Rider, a terrific new publication for kids.

Munchy Crunchy Christmas Cake

Ingredients:

Magic Christmas Munchy Mixture

Parsnip or carrot,
    cut in finger-length pieces

Bread crumbs (make these by putting two
    slices of bread into a blender)

Lifesaver mints, peppermint candy
    or seedless red grapes

Parsley, celery leaves or carrot tops

ill a large bowl with Magic Christmas Munchy Mixture and mix in a sliced parsnip or carrot. Press this mixture into a cake pan you've greased and pack as tightly as you can. Cover the cake pan with a plate and flip over. Tap the pan with a spoon and gently lift the pan off the cake.

To garnish: Sprinkle with bread crumbs. Decorate top with Lifesavers or peppermints. If your horse bolts his feed, top with red seedless grapes. Add a carrot candle if you like and some parsley, celery leaves or carrot tops around the base of the cake.   ♥

Contributed of Lesley Ward and Young Rider Magazine.

Photo contributed by Bonnie Kreitler. © Kreitler Media Services

Majesty's Mellowcreme Treats

Ingredients:

2 tablespoons margarine

20 marshmallows

2 cups sweet feed

1 cup cracked corn
} You may substitute all sweet feed or all oats.

1/2 cup mellowcreme treats

    (such as candy corn, pumpkins,

    santas, etc.)

1/2 cup bran

Photo contributed by Stephanie Macejko.

 ightly grease with margarine an 8 x 8 cake pan and dust with bran. Set aside.

Melt margarine in a 4-quart saucepan over medium heat. Add marshmallows gradually, stirring constantly until melted. Remove from heat and add sweet feed, cracked corn and candy (candy corn, pumpkins, etc.). Stir well until coated. Transfer into the cake pan, dust the top with bran and press down. Cool and cut into squares. Dust with more bran. ♥

Contributed by Stephanie Macejko. Stephanie is the Editor of Just About Horses, *a unique publication for Breyer Animal Creations. Breyer is famous for its model horses and animals.*

30-Second Right Side Up Cake

Ingredients:

2 cups oats
1 cup sweet feed
Handful alfalfa leaves
Few tufts of Broome hay heads

 ix the oats and sweet feed together and pour into feed bucket. Sprinkle the alfalfa leaves over the mixture and arrange the Broome hay heads on top. Serve immediately. *Quickie garnish:* Place a handful of raisins in the center. ♥

Contributed by Ann Gilbertson of Saskatchewan, Canada. Ann mentions that she arranges a ribbon and bow around the dish for birthdays. See Decorative Garnishes, for terrific edible ribbons.

Grass Sheet Cake

Ingredients:

Grass seed
Potting Soil
Gravel or sand
Apple, sliced
Carrots, cut in 3 inch pieces

 ut about 1/2 to 1 inch of gravel or sand at the bottom of a baking pan with 2-3 inch sides. Lay 1 to 2 inches of potting soil on top and plant the grass seed. Water with a sprayer to avoid disturbing seeds or crushing the delicate new grass. Wait one month.

To garnish: Arrange carrots and apple slices in a circle on top of grass. Don't worry about the dirt; your horse will shake that out himself. This is an especially nice treat if grown indoors in winter, as it is a terrific reminder of spring. ♥

Contributed by Kristine Gunther of Milwaukee, WI. Kristine owns Windmere Mystic Lady, a bay Morab (half Morgan and half Arabian), and lives on her farm, Mystic Meadows. Kristine frequently writes for many horse magazines.

Birthday Cones

Ingredients:

- Wafer ice cream cones
- 1 apple, shredded
- 1 carrot, shredded
- 1/2 cup brown sugar
- 1/2 cup dark corn syrup
- 1 cup bran
- Seedless green or red grapes
- Confectionery sugar

 ix apple, carrot, brown sugar and corn syrup thoroughly. Add bran to make the mixture thick and paste-like, adding more bran as needed. Using a greased ice cream scoop, scoop balls of mixture into wafer cones. *To garnish:* Top each with one grape and sprinkle with confectionery sugar. ♥

Brainstormed by Liz Hoskinson of New York City, NY and June Evers.

Watermelon Birthday Cake

Ingredients:

- 1 medium-size watermelon
- Sweet feed or oats
- Carrots
    - Serve as many carrots as your horse is years old

lice watermelon crosswise (retaining rind and seeds) into circular 2-inch slices and stack large slices at the bottom, small ones at the top. Ice with sweet feed or oats. Cut carrots into strips and stick them into the exposed watermelon slices. ♥

Contributed by Nanci Falley, President of the American Indian Horse Registry, Inc. of Lockhart, TX. Nanci says this is a 35-year-old favorite at her farm.

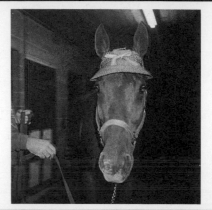

Birthday Apparel. Top: Pam's Pleasure posing in her favorite hat. Above: Pam's Pleasure in a tutu. Her owner, Pam Farrior, handmade a ballet tutu for Pam's Pleasure to wear complete with a crown. (Some horses have such terrific dispositions. Only try this if your horse is as easy going as Pam's horse is.) Photo contributed by Pamela S. Farrior, R.Ph. Pam owns Broad Axe Pharmacy & Broad Axe Horse Supplies, a division of Broad Axe Pharmacy of Ambler, PA.

Upside Down Layer Cake

Ingredients:

- 1 cup sweet feed
- 1 cup oats
- 2 cups bran
- Brown sugar
- Molasses
- 5 carrots, sliced
- Confectionery sugar

enerously grease a large round cake pan and set aside.

In a separate bowl, mix 1/2 cup molasses and 1/2 cup brown sugar. (Mixture should be very thick, so add more brown sugar if necessary.) Pour into cake pan and press sliced carrots flat into mixture, arranging pieces around the pan's perimeter. Pour the sweet feed on in a layer (you are starting your layer cake) and smooth it out flat. Dribble 1 cup of molasses over that.

In a separate bowl, mix 2 cups bran and about 2 cups molasses together. It should have a thick consistency. Use more or less bran and molasses depending on your pan size. Pour a layer of this mixture into cake pan on top of sweet feed layer. It should be about 1/2 inch thick. (*Use only half of what you've prepared*, as you'll need the rest later.) Add oats as the next layer to cake and smooth out. Then pour another 1/2 to 1 cup of molasses onto oats. Top off with the remainder of the bran/molasses mixture. Put in the freezer overnight.

To remove: Carefully flip pan over and let cake gradually drop by itself onto a plate placed underneath.

To garnish: Sprinkle a handful of oats and 1 to 2 tablespoons of confectionery sugar on top of cake. Slice and serve while cool. ♥

Contributed by T. Redding of Summit, NJ. She says her horse Ridgewood (Reggie), loves this treat on birthdays. She also mentions that this is an especially gooey treat, so don't let it sit too long—it will melt and run all over!

**THIS IS A VERY RICH RECIPE,
SO CUT CAKE IN SLICES
AND SERVE TO SEVERAL HORSES.
DON'T FEED JUST ONE!**

Mom's Apple Spice Muffins

Ingredients:

- 1 cup flour
- 1 cup wheat germ
- 1/2 teaspoon cinnamon
- 1/2 cup sugar
- 1/2 teaspoon salt
- 3 teaspoons baking powder
- 1 egg
- 2/3 cup milk
- 1/4 cup corn oil
- 1 cup apples (Macintosh), chopped

Mystery gallops by, outside Cheyenne, Wyoming. Mystery is known from the upcoming Mystery Series, Mystery of Lonetree Cemetery.

reheat oven to 400 degrees. Generously grease muffin tins.

In a large bowl, mix dry ingredients together and set aside. In a separate bowl, mix thoroughly the remaining ingredients including the apples. Then, pour the liquid ingredients into the dry ingredients. Mix until everything is moistened. Scoop into muffin tins and bake 15 to 25 minutes. Serve cool to horses. Serve warm to people! ♥

Contributed by Helen & Bill Evers of Goshen, NY. Everyone enjoys this terrific recipe up at the Evers farm, both horses and people. Super for Christmas morning.

Pop Pop's Scooter romps in his paddock. Photo contributed by Jim Kersbergen.

Los Gatos Bite-Sized Cookies

Ingredients:

2 cups rolled oats

1 cup cracked corn

1 cup flax seed

1 cup wheat

1 cup rolled barley

1 tablespoon salt

1 cup oat bran

1 cup wheat bran

6 cups Quaker Oats

2 1/2 cups applesauce

2 1/4 cups molasses

2 cups hot water

rease a large cookie sheet lightly and set aside.

Use a 5-quart container which can be covered while refrigerated. Mix all ingredients well and refrigerate batter covered for one hour before baking.

Using a tablespoon, scoop each cookie onto a cookie sheet and flatten slightly. Bake at 275 degrees for 45 minutes, then turn cookies over and bake an additional 45 minutes. Makes 17 dozen bite-sized cookies. ❤

Contributed by Ann Parks of Los Gatos, CA.

Super Storing:

THE BAKED COOKIES LAST SEVERAL WEEKS AS LONG AS THEY ARE STORED IN A CLEAN, DRY PLACE. EXTRA COOKIES CAN BE STORED IN THE FREEZER AND TAKEN OUT AS NEEDED.

REFRIGERATED BATTER KEEPS ABOUT TWO DAYS.

Caramel Corn Clusters

Ingredients:

- 1 cup cracked corn
- 1 cup granulated sugar
- 1 tablespoon brown sugar
- Water

preheat oven to 350 degrees and grease cookie sheet. Mix ingredients together. Add only enough water so mixture clings together. Mixture will be crumbly. Onto cookie sheet, mound mixture into piles about 2-inches in size. Bake for 10 to 15 minutes. Let cool for 1 hour. Use a spatula to scrape clusters off cookie sheet. ❤

FOR EASY NO-COOK CLUSTERS: ADD MOLASSES, INSTEAD OF WATER, AND REFRIGERATE OVERNIGHT. THEN SERVE IMMEDIATELY!

Sundae Supreme

Ingredients:

- 1/4 cup oats
- 1/4 cup sweet feed
- 3/4 cup bran
- 1 1/4 cup molasses
- 1 cup brown sugar
- 1 apple, cut in small cubes
- 1 carrot, diced 1/4 inch
- 1 wafer cone dish (the kind used to make sundaes)
- 1 piece of peppermint candy or a seedless green or red grape.

mix the oats, sweet feed and bran. Add 1/2 cup brown sugar and 3/4 cup molasses and mix. Mixture should be thick enough so it can be easily shaped and molded. Set aside.

In a separate bowl, mix thoroughly another 1/2 cup molasses, and 1/2 cup more brown sugar, add carrots and apple cubes. Mixture should be runny. Pour into the bottom of the wafer cone dish and smooth out with a spoon.

Scoop the oat, sweet feed and bran mixture into the wafer cone dish and cover the carrot and apple mixture. Mold this into a mound.

To garnish: Drip more molasses over the top and place a peppermint in the center. If your horse bolts his feed, use a seedless green or red grape instead. Limit one cone dish per horse. ❤

THIS IS A VERY RICH RECIPE, SO SERVE ONLY ONE WAFER CONE PER HORSE!

Applesauce Horse Cookies

Ingredients:

1 cup sweet feed

2 to 3 cups bran

1 cup flax seed

1 tablespoon salt

4 large carrots, shredded

1 cup molasses

1/2 cup brown sugar

1 cup applesauce

Herding cattle near Cody, Wyoming, a cow pony waits his turn.

mix the molasses, brown sugar, carrots and applesauce in one bowl. In another, mix the dry ingredients. Slowly combine the molasses mixture with the dry ingredients. Add only enough molasses mixture to form a thick dough. Add more bran if necessary.

Line cookie sheet with aluminum foil. Using a tablespoon, drop batter onto cookie sheet and flatten slightly to form portions about the size of a silver dollar. Bake at 300 degrees for 1 hour, flip cookies over and bake an additional 45 minutes until they are dried out. Just keep checking to make sure they don't burn. ❤

Based on a recipe by Rebecca Yocum of Mt. Bethel, PA.

Microwave Peanut Brittle

Ingredients:

1 cup sugar

1/2 cup corn syrup

1 1/2 cups rolled oats

1/2 cup corn meal

1 cup bran

1 teaspoon butter or margarine

1 teaspoon baking soda

ightly grease a cookie sheet and set aside. In a microwave-safe container, stir together sugar and syrup. Microwave on high for 4 minutes. **CAUTION: THE SYRUP GETS VERY HOT AND MAY SPATTER!** Take out and carefully stir in dry ingredients until mixture is dry and crumbly. Microwave again on high for 3 to 5 minutes. Remove and stir in butter. **AGAIN, CAREFUL!** Microwave a third time on high 1 to 2 minutes. Add baking soda quickly to mixture and pour onto greased cookie sheet. Flatten with greased spoon. Score brittle with knife or pizza cutter into 1 inch by 2 inch squares. When mixture is cool, break apart along scores and store in an airtight container.

Mixture must reach 300 degrees to create the hard crack stage. Undercooking will result in a chewy, sticky biscuit. You can reheat mixture for up to 4 minutes to reach the hard crack stage. ♥

Contributed by Kelinda Sloan of Nova Scotia, Canada.

CANDY MIXTURE REACHES APPROXIMATELY 300 DEGREES, SO USE EXTREME CAUTION WHEN HANDLING MIXTURE. ADULT SUPERVISION IS RECOMMENDED!

Granola Balls

Ingredients:

1/2 cup rolled oats

1/4 cup bran

1 heaping tablespoon sugar

1 tablespoon molasses

1 tablespoon honey

1 tablespoon water

ombine oats, bran, sugar, molasses and honey, mixing thoroughly. Add water until consistency is thick and moist, but not drippy. Refrigerate dough 1 hour. Form dough into golf-ball-sized lumps. To keep dough from sticking to your hands, wipe hands lightly with corn oil. Feed immediately. ♥

Contributed by Valerie Zink of Alberta, Canada.

Photo contributed by Valerie Zink of Alberta, Canada.

Photo contributed by Erin Appleyard of Ontario, Canada.

Britches, who is especially fond of his post-workout snacks. Photo contributed by Liz Hoskinson of New York City, NY.

Carrot Bran Cups

Ingredients:

2 cups flour

1/2 cup sugar

2 cups bran

1 carrot, grated

2 cups water

1 tablespoon soft butter or margarine

1 teaspoon baking powder

1 teaspoon baking soda

Preheat oven to 350 degrees. Generously grease a muffin tin. Set aside.

In a large bowl, stir in flour, sugar, bran, grated carrot, baking powder and baking soda. Add butter and water. Mix well and scoop into muffin tin. Bake for 25 to 35 minutes or until toothpick comes out clean. Makes six muffins. ♥

Contributed by Laurie Fogus of Calimesa, CA.

Carrot Bran Glaze

Ingredients:

1 cup flour

2 cups confectionery sugar

1/2 cup bran

1 carrot, grated

Water

mix the dry ingredients with the carrot. Add water until you reach a desired consistency. Spread over Carrot Bran Cups. ♥

Contributed by Laurie Fogus of Calimesa, CA. Laurie says her horses love these cupcakes.

Cabaret, after a competition. Photo contributed by Karen Ufret of Port Jervis, NY.

Decorative Garnishes

Decorative Garnishes

GREAT CANDY GARNISHES:

If you horse tends to eat too quickly, feed the mushier garnishes on page 63.

PEPPERMINTS

JELLY BEANS

CANDY CORN

LIFESAVERS

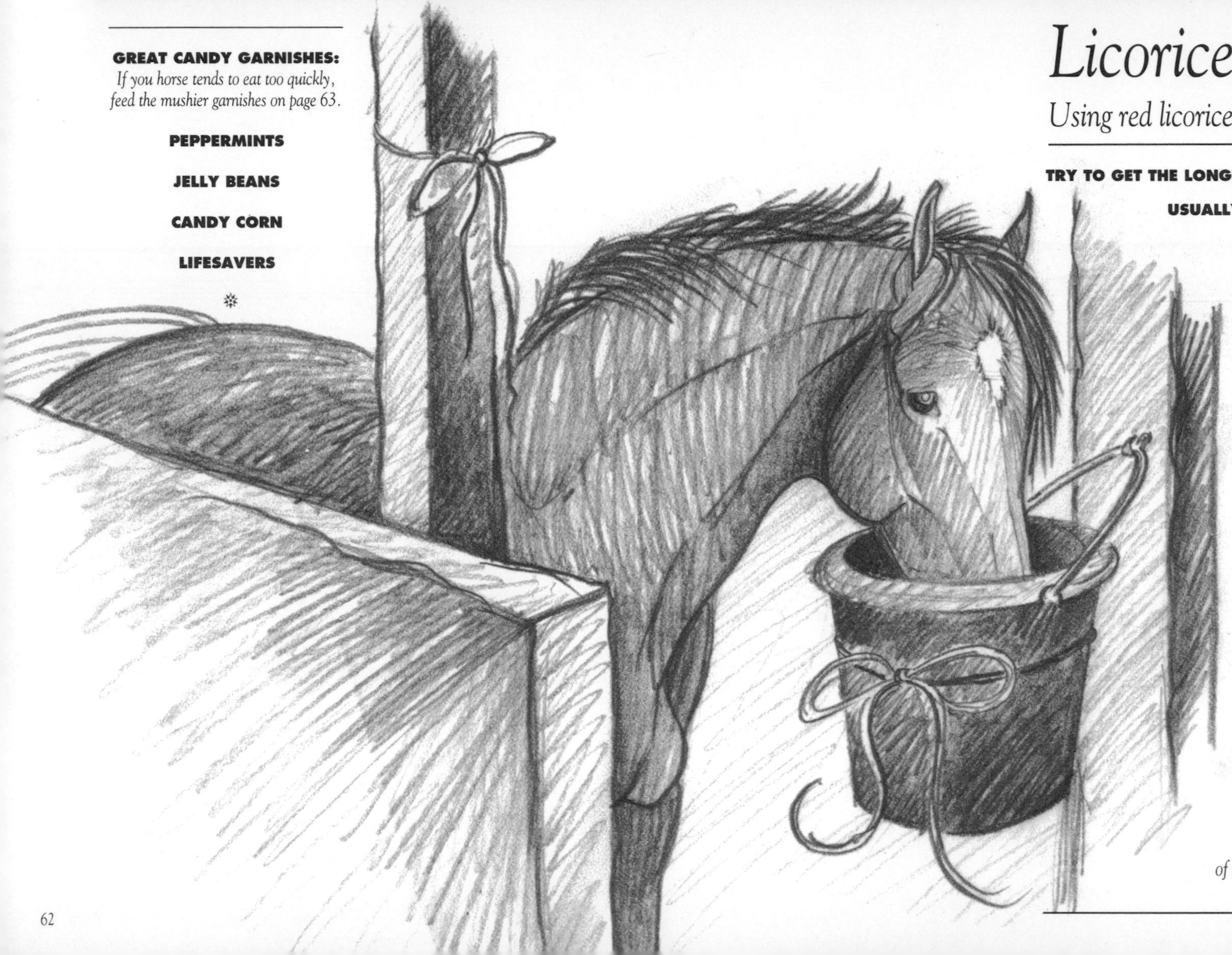

Licorice Bows

Using red licorice, the very thin kind:

TRY TO GET THE LONGEST STRANDS OF LICORICE, USUALLY AVAILABLE IN SPECIALTY CANDY STORES.

SIMPLY WRAP IT AROUND YOUR FAVORITE TREAT AND TIE WITH A BOW.

ANOTHER IDEA: TIE STRANDS TO AN ACCESSIBLE BEAM ABOUT 4 FEET OFF THE GROUND IN HORSE'S STALL, WHERE HE CAN NIBBLE IT OFF WHEN HE FINDS IT. OR SIMPLY TIE AROUND A FEED BUCKET.

*Contributed by Linda Stark
of Gramercy Park, New York City.*

Apple Roses

Using one Red Delicious apple:

USING A KNIFE OR POTATO PEELER, CAREFULLY
PEEL SKIN SLOWLY OFF APPLE IN ONE
CONTINUOUS SPIRAL STRING.

FOLLOWING DIAGRAMS BELOW AND AT RIGHT,
ARRANGE PEEL IN A CIRCLE TO MAKE A ROSE.
FOR ADDED COLOR, PLACE A RED SEEDLESS
GRAPE IN THE CENTER.

THIS GARNISH IS VERY FRAGILE, MAKE
DIRECTLY ON BRAN MASH
OR SPECIAL TREAT.

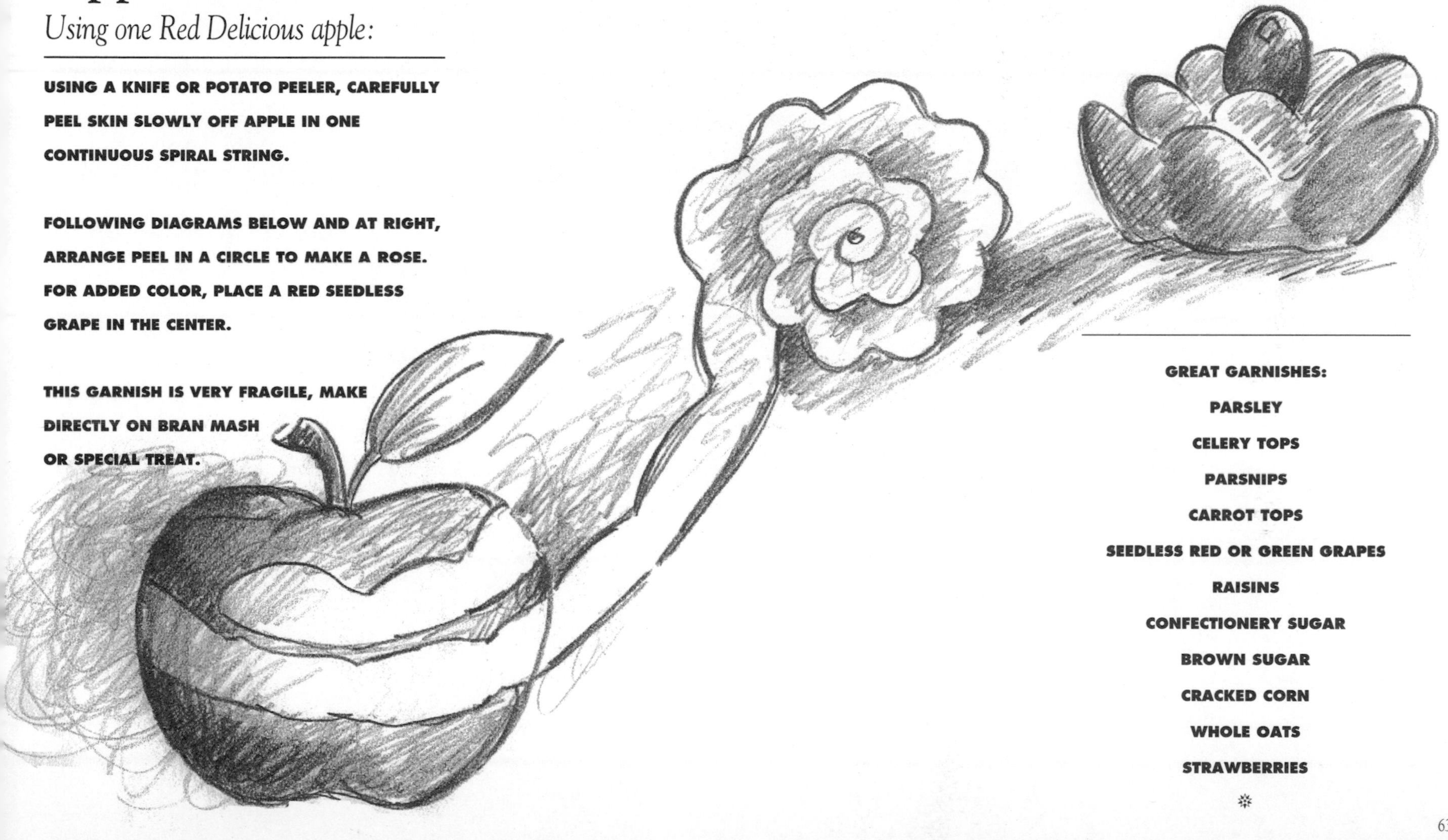

GREAT GARNISHES:

PARSLEY

CELERY TOPS

PARSNIPS

CARROT TOPS

SEEDLESS RED OR GREEN GRAPES

RAISINS

CONFECTIONERY SUGAR

BROWN SUGAR

CRACKED CORN

WHOLE OATS

STRAWBERRIES

❋

Photo contributed by Sallie A. Scoggin of Chicago, IL.

Nutritional & Grooming Hints

Rainy Monday morning at Lake Erie College. Photo contributed by Sallie A. Scoggin of Chicago, IL.

Electrolytes

Ingredients:

1 16 ounce container of table salt

2 11 ounce container Morton Lite Salt

2 tablespoons Epsom salts

mix all ingredients together thoroughly. Dose: Use 1 1/2 tablespoons of electrolyte mix. You can place on top of grain.

If the horse needs a quick boost, mix 1 dose electrolytes with 4 tablespoons pancake syrup and 4 tablespoons lukewarm water. Put in a large syringe and squirt in the horse's mouth.

Note: When using electrolytes of any kind, fresh water must be available at all times. ♥

Contributed by Kathy Andrews, Hunter Cross Farm of Reidsville, NC. Kathy's husband, Bill Andrews, teaches dressage and is the North Carolina State Director for the American Warmblood Society.

Cider Vinegar:

FEED 2 OUNCES OF CIDER VINEGAR TWICE DAILY FOR VITAMIN C. THIS HELPS STIMULATE APPETITE AND BALANCE THE IMMUNE SYSTEM. USE GOOD CIDER VINEGAR FROM A HEALTH FOOD STORE, NOT THE CARAMEL COLORED VINEGAR USUALLY FOUND IN MOST SUPERMARKETS!

Contributed by Susie L. Johnson of Nags 'n Rags, Inc. a store located both in Enumclaw, WA and Lexington, KY. She says that this is an old horseman's remedy that she still uses today.

Raw Eggs:

BEAT 1 TO 3 EGGS WELL AND STIR INTO GRAIN ONCE A DAY FOR A SHINY COAT. BECAUSE THE OLD EGG MIXTURE WILL ATTRACT FLIES AND FLY EGGS, MAKE SURE TO CLEAN THE FEED BUCKET THOROUGHLY AFTER EVERY FEEDING!

Garlic:

IF YOUR HORSE RUBS ITS TAIL, FEED ONE CLOVE OF GARLIC DAILY. CRUSH IT INTO THE BRAN MASH, FEED IN A SALAD OR PLACE WHOLE WITHIN APPLESAUCE BUTE LUMPS *(see page 71).*

Contributed by Liz Gray, a horse farm specialist for Century 21, Las Vegas, NV. Gladys Bernstein, of Fort Lee, NJ, mixes garlic in with a bran mash.

Author's Note: In compiling this book, I received several letters praising the benefits of garlic! It is believed to combat parasites that usually cause a horse to rub its tail. Of course, I still strongly reccommend that you have your horse wormed regularly—by your veterinarian or with a commercial wormer.

Author's Note: If you decide to try eggs, start gradually as with all new feeds and treats, BUT ALSO, stay on top of cleaning the feed bucket after every feeding with eggs.

Listerine Sweat

Ingredients:

Listerine

Cotton bandages & standing wraps

Saran Wrap

apply Listerine generously to your horses legs, rubbing gently. Bandage legs with cotton wraps while they are still wet. Next, cover cotton bandages by wrapping Saran Wrap completely around. Then wrap with standing wraps as usual. The sweat should NOT be tight, but should be snug enough to stay up overnight. ♥

This is an old racetrack remedy for "stocked up" legs and can be used as a refreshing brace after a strenuous workout. ("Stocked up,"incidentally, is a horseman's term for describing legs that are slightly swollen. Active horses confined to stalls sometimes become stocked up overnight due to lack of exercise.)

Liniment

Ingredients:

2 pints clear alcohol

2 pints wintergreen alcohol

2 pints witch hazel

1/2 bottle store-bought equine liniment

pour all ingredients in a clean gallon container. If there is room, top off with white vinegar. Rub onto horse's legs and bandage. ♥

Contributed by Kathy Andrews of Reidsville, NC.

Homemade Hoof Care

Ingredients:

1 gallon lanolin

1 gallon pine tar

mix 1 gallon lanolin and 1 gallon pine tar in a large container. Apply to hooves twice daily when they are dry. ♥

Contributed by Ron and Serge Massolin, Serge's Tack Shop in Ontario, Canada.

WHOA!

THESE ARE TERRIFIC TREATMENTS <u>FOR</u> HORSES,

THEY SHOULD NOT BE FED TO HORSES!

Grooming Hints

DeAnn's Mane & Tail Detangler

Ingredients:

Calgon Bath Oil Beads (dry)
Water

mix the Calgon with water (one part Calgon to 3 parts water) in a spray bottle. Spray on mane and tail to help recondition. Also works well on knots: apply liberally and work out knot with a comb or stiff brush. ♥

Contributed by DeAnn Parks Schott of Costa Mesa, CA. DeAnn, a licensed horse appraiser and certified equine masseuse, is frequently known as DeAnn Doolittle for her love of all animals.

So many enthusiasts wrote to us about the benefits of Calgon to help ease knots, we just had to include it.

Fly Spray

Ingredients:

2 cups white vinegar
1 cup Avon Skin So Soft Bath Oil (Original Scent)
1 cup water
1 tablespoon eucalyptus oil (available at health food stores)

mix ingredients together in a spray bottle. Apply to your horse before riding or turning out. It will wear off as your horse sweats, so reapply as needed. ♥

Contributed by George Venables of Reseda, CA. A surprising number of people suggested recipes for fly spray — and specified Avon Skin So Soft.

Heel Scratch Preparation

Ingredients:

Glycerin
Cider vinegar

mix equal amounts in a container you can cover. Rub on heel scratches twice daily until cured. ♥

Contributed by Dewaine Moore of Rainier Stables, Enumclaw, WA. This is an old remedy used for many years at the racetrack.

White Vinegar:

MIX 1 CUP WHITE VINEGAR TO 1 GALLON WATER. USE AS AN AFTER-WORKOUT COOL-DOWN BATH AND LINIMENT.

Contributed by Kathy Andrews of Hunter Cross Farm, Reidsville, NC.

Dr. Z's Magic Mild Colic Elixir

Ingredients:

4 cups mineral oil

1 cup cheap wine

Dash ground Cayenne pepper

or ginger

mix ingredients thoroughly and administer orally to your horse with several doses from a large basting syringe. Walk the horse for half an hour or so to prevent him from lying down and rolling.

If the horse fails to show improvement, *call the veterinarian immediately!* ♥

Contributed by Linda Lewin of Zapopan, Mexico. Linda notes that it is important to keep the ingredients on hand as it is particularly embarrassing to rush to the grocery or liquor store at 9:00 a.m. in a panic to buy cheap wine. She says the cashiers tend to give you a funny look especially when you try to convince them that it IS for your horse, and not for you!! This recipe was given to her by a veterinarian from Georgia many years ago.

Mrs. Adams' Wild West Colic Cure

Ingredients:

2 cups brewed black coffee

1 cup cheap whiskey

this recipe dates back to about 1930 — and perhaps even earlier. Mix warm black coffee and whiskey together. Using a basting syringe, squirt solution into the back of your horses mouth — then walk him to prevent him from lying down and rolling. ♥

This was taught to me by the late Mrs. Sheila Adams of South Salem, NY. Mrs. Adams, a horsewoman for over 50 years, many of her methods were based on longstanding folk remedies.

WHOA! *Authors Note: While these colic remedies have been used successfully over the years by Dr. Z, Linda Lewin and Mrs. Sheila Adams, they are not offered as substitutes for experienced veterinary care. I recommend that you call your veterinarian any time your horse shows signs of colic, and that you always consult with your veterinarian before administering these or other homemade colic remedies.*

Applesauce Bute Lumps

Ingredients:

- 1/2 cup applesauce
- 1 to 2 cups Quaker Oats
- 3 to 4 tablespoons sugar
- 1 tablespoon molasses

mix ingredients together and add enough Quaker Oats to form a thick paste. Keeps about 10 days in the refrigerator. When you are ready to medicate your horse, scoop out a spoonful, big enough to bury the bute pill. You can break the pill in half or you can bury the *whole* pill within the lump.

For added garnish: Coat the lump by dropping in a baggie filled with Quaker Oats. To keep your hands clean, insert the pill after placing lump in bag. Squeeze pill into lump through plastic.

Since bute pills are bitter and dissolve quickly, don't add them until you are ready to medicate—usually right outside the stall.

A final suggestion: Feed your horse one lump without the bute pill, a second with the pill, and a third without. He'll assume he's receiving nothing but treats! ♥

Contributed by Liz Gray, a horse farm specialist for Century 21, Aaimheigh, Las Vegas, NV.

Tough Time Medicating Your Horse?

Here are some terrific ways to medicate your horse, especially if the medication is bitter. For the recipes within this box, make sure medication is in liquid or powdered form (crush pills to form a powder.) If you want to store the recipes, store **WITHOUT** the medication. Add medication only immediately **BEFORE** feeding.

MIX MEDICATION THOROUGHLY WITH KARO OR PANCAKE SYRUP (OR MOLASSES AND BROWN SUGAR MIXED). PUT THIS MIXTURE DIRECTLY ON TOP OF REGULAR FEED OR USE A BIG SYRINGE AND SQUIRT IT IN YOUR HORSE'S MOUTH.

Contributed by Kristi Pigg of Lena, MS.

...OR TRY MIXING MEDICATION WITH 1/2 TEASPOON MOLASSES AND 2 TEASPOONS SECOND STAGE BABY FOOD CARROTS. AGAIN, PUT MIXTURE DIRECTLY ON TOP OF REGULAR FEED OR USE A SYRINGE AND SQUIRT IN YOUR HORSE'S MOUTH.

Contributed by Laurie McKeown, Yale Creek Ranch of Jacksonville, OR. Laurie mentions her horse, Razz, likes this concoction so much he will lick it out of the bowl.

...OR HOW ABOUT MIXING A TEASPOON OF RASPBERRY JELLO POWDER WITH THE MEDICATION AND WATER.

Contributed by Meredith Morrell, West Wind Appaloosa Sport Horses of Rising Sun, MD. Meredith was the owner of the late First Secretary, Secretariat's first foal out of Leola.

Do you have any

homemade recipes,

grooming tips,

remedies,

homemade horse costumes or clothing,

unique tricks you've

taught your horse,

or just comments you'd like to share?

Drop us a note!

HORSE HOLLOW PRESS
P.O. Box 456, Goshen, NY 10924-0456

Call or write for our free catalog of
unique new products for horse lovers!

Order more copies!

VISIT YOUR FAVORITE TACK & FEED, BOOK, OR GIFT STORE!

Or send $19.95 per copy plus $4.50 shipping and packing to Horse Hollow Press. (Add $1.50 per additional book ordered for shipping and packing).

Mail to: HORSE HOLLOW PRESS
P.O. Box 456
Goshen, NY 10924-0456

Yes! Please send me [qty.] _____ copy (ies) of THE ORIGINAL BOOK OF HORSE TREATS at $19.95. I have included $4.50 for shipping & packing for the first book, $1.50 per additional book. **Total enclosed: $_____**
(Check, money order, or credit cards accepted.)
OR CALL TOLL-FREE: 1-800-4-1-HORSE to order!

Name: _____

Address: _____

City/State/Zip: _____

Phone: _____

Visa/MC: _____ Exp. Date: _____

Signature: _____